Napoleon

Alan Blackwood

Illustrations by Richard Hook

Great Lives

William Shakespeare
Queen Elizabeth II
Anne Frank
Martin Luther King
Helen Keller
Ferdinand Magellan
Mother Teresa
Louis Braille
John Lennon

John F. Kennedy
Florence Nightingale
Elvis Presley
Gandhi
Captain Cook
Napoleon
Einstein
Beethoven
Marie Curie

First published in 1986 by
Wayland (Publishers) Limited
61 Western Road, Hove
East Sussex BN3 1JD, England

© Copyright 1986 Wayland (Publishers) Limited

British Library Cataloguing in Publication Data
Blackwood, Alan
  Napoleon.—(Great lives)
  1. Napoleon I, *Emperor of the French*
  Juvenile literature   2. France—Kings
  and rulers—Biography—Juvenile
  literature
  I. Title   II. Hook, Richard   III. Series
  944.05′092′4   DC203

ISBN 0 85078 890 0

Phototypeset by The Bath Press, Avon
Printed and Bound in Italy by G. Canale & C.S.p.A., Turin

Contents

Birth and revolution

In 1768 the Italian city of Genoa surrendered the Mediterranean island of Corsica to France. Just one year later, on 15 August 1769, Napoleon Buonaparte was born on the island, one of a family of eight children. Young Napoleon went to military schools in France. His classmates often laughed at the rather rough-looking boy from Corsica. But despite their mockery he studied hard, proving especially good at mathematics and

At school, Napoleon's French classmates teased him because he was a Corsican.

gunnery, and at 16 years of age he joined an artillery regiment as an officer cadet.

In 1789, the French Revolution began. The people of Paris tore down the hated old Bastille prison. The new government executed King Louis XVI and Queen Marie-Antoinette and declared France a republic. The other monarchies of Europe, notably Britain, Prussia and the

King Louis XVI was executed and France was declared a republic.

Austrian Empire, were shocked and frightened by these events, the more so as France was a strong country at that time with the largest population in western Europe. They declared war on the new French Republic, planning to attack and destroy it.

At 24, Napoleon became a captain of artillery. He was just the kind of soldier France needed at that moment in her history. For Napoleon, the events of the time could not have been better. In ten years he would rise to become the most powerful man in the world.

Love and war

Napoleon directing the cannon fire against the royalist uprising.

Napoleon's first opportunity to gain recognition came in 1793. A royalist force, backed by the British navy, had captured Toulon, France's chief naval base in the Mediterranean. The young artillery captain from Corsica was called in to help the republicans. In pouring rain he led a daring attack against the British ships in the harbour. The royalists were forced to leave the town. Napoleon was immediately promoted to the rank of brigadier.

Napoleon had another chance to prove his worth two years later, when royalists staged an uprising in Paris. Napoleon again put his artillery to good use, killing or dispersing the royalists. The grateful government promoted him once more, to the rank of general.

At this time Napoleon met and fell in love with Josephine Beauharnais. They married in March 1796. Two days later he left for Nice, to command the army in Italy.

Napoleon led his troops in an attack on the Austrian Empire's north Italian provinces. Using tactics of swift movement and surprise, he captured Turin and Milan, and in January 1797 defeated the bulk of the Austrian army at Rivoli.

This was Napoleon's first major victory. He cleverly arranged a quick peace, before any reinforcements could come to Austria's aid.

Napoleon fell in love with Josephine Beauharnais. Two days after their wedding, he had to leave for Italy.

To Egypt and back

Part of the French fleet was destroyed by Nelson at the Battle of the Nile.

Young Napoleon, full of confidence and ambition, told the French government (the Directory) what to do next. 'In order to destroy Britain,' he said, 'we must seize Egypt.' By so doing, he argued, they would cut off Britain's vital trade links with India and the Far East. At the same time this would draw a large part of the British navy away from home waters, so making it possible to invade Britain herself. The Directory agreed, and put him in charge of a new army.

Napoleon landed his army in Egypt in June 1798, managing to

avoid a British naval squadron commanded by Admiral Nelson. 'Forty centuries look down on us,' he told his troops as they took up positions near the famous pyramids. Despite the blazing heat and dust they put to flight the army of the Mamluks, Egypt's ruling dynasty.

Ten days later, Nelson caught up with part of the French fleet and destroyed it at anchor in Aboukir Bay, off the coast of Egypt. Napoleon defiantly went ahead with his plans for turning Egypt into a French colony. He instituted new forms of government and finance, and cleaned up the streets of Cairo and Alexandria. He had also taken with him some important scholars, whom he put to work studying the marvels of Egypt's ancient past.

All the same, the destruction of the French fleet wrecked Napoleon's military plans. After repulsing a Turkish force backed by the British in Syria, he decided to cut his losses and return home, leaving most of his army behind.

Napoleon took several famous scholars to Egypt to investigate the contents of the ancient pyramids.

The First Consul

Napoleon timed his return well. His Egyptian campaign may have failed, but France was threatened by a new coalition of European powers, and the French people were glad to see him home again. He judged the time ripe to make a bid for political power.

Backed by the cunning and clever Foreign Minister, Charles de Talleyrand, and by the army, he took over the Directory. Then he drew up a new constitution, proposing a government called the Consulate, with himself at its head as First Consul. Correctly judging the mood of the nation, he secured popular support for his constitution in a referendum. In 1800, the first year of a new century, he became the new leader of France.

Napoleon first turned his attention to urgent military matters. He decided to personally lead another army back into Italy, to repeat his earlier triumphs against the Austrians.

In May 1800, he and his army

crossed the Alps from Switzerland into Italy by the great St Bernard Pass. They were held up by the problem of getting heavy cannon over the icy, rocky pass, and by stubborn enemy resistance. Then, in June, they had to face a powerful Austrian army at the Battle of Marengo, on the north Italian plain. They won, but only just.

Napoleon's victory at Marengo confirmed his political power at home.

Above Charles de Talleyrand, Napoleon's clever Foreign Minister, who eventually forced Napoleon to abdicate.

Below The French Army crossing the treacherous Alps with fierce determination.

The Code Napoléon

Napoleon had already shown a flair for administration. Back in Paris, as First Consul, he proved himself as much a genius in government as on the battlefield.

The Revolution was over, he said, and it was time for France to have a strong and stable government. He appointed people to oversee different areas of France which were to be run according to central government policy. He created a state educational system, allowing the most talented from all classes of the community to better themselves, and a central bank to control the nation's finances.

Napoleon draws up the Code Napoléon *stating the rights and duties of his citizens.*

He also laid down a new civil and legal code; the *Code Napoléon* which stated the rights and duties of all citizens. By these methods, Napoleon created the blueprint for most modern systems of government and law.

Napoleon also acted very shrewdly. The Revolution had got rid of the Church in France. But Napoleon knew that most French people still wanted their

Napoleon created the Legion of Honour medal, which is still awarded today.

Napoleon became the First Consul of France in 1800.

old religion. So he restored the Church but brought in government controls over it. He also created a new system of bestowing honours for achievement called the Legion of Honour.

In March 1802, Napoleon added to his success by signing a peace treaty with Britain. His popularity was at its peak. He had made France the best-governed country in the world, and brought peace. A grateful nation made him First Consul for life.

Emperor of France

The peace did not last for long. The British had for centuries been concerned with protecting their own interests by trying to prevent any one European country from dominating the rest. A hundred years before, the British had helped to stop the domination of continental Europe by the French King Louis XIV. Now France under Napoleon seemed to be intent on the same course. She was reluctant to give up those territories beyond France, so recently won in battle. Moreover, the French were increasingly active overseas, threatening Britain's own world trade. They were also laying claim to a part of the newly discovered land of Australia, which they called Napoleon's land. By May 1803, after just a year of peace, the two nations were at war again.

Napoleon responded with the most sensational act of his career. He decided to create a new ruling dynasty in France, so that even if he were killed, the Napoleonic state would continue. On 2 December 1804, at a magnificent ceremony in Notre Dame Cathedral, Paris, he had himself crowned Emperor of the French, dramatically placing a crown on his own head. He had already changed the Italian spelling of the family name Buonaparte to the more French-sounding Bonaparte. Now he dropped the name altogether. Henceforth he was to be known as Napoleon I.

The extent of the Napoleonic Empire in 1812.

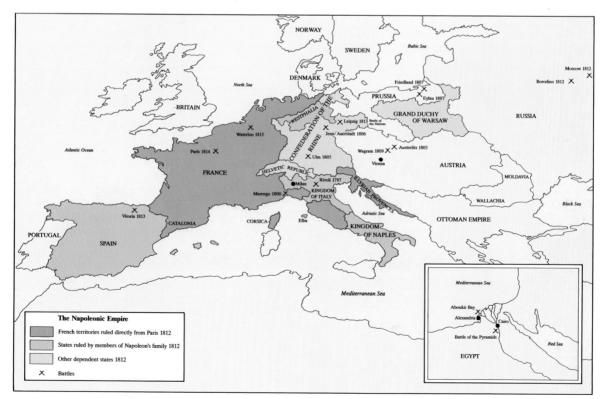

The greatest victory

Napoleon had gorgeous robes for his coronation, but for most of the time he now wore the familiar broad black hat, green jacket or grey coat, white breeches and black boots, which set him apart from his marshals and ministers in their more splendid uniforms.

He planned to invade Britain, and in the spring of 1805 he assembled an army of nearly 140,000 men at Boulogne on the Channel coast, looking across the Straits of Dover. He hoped his admirals would lure the British navy far out into the Atlantic Ocean, so that his army could make the crossing in safety. 'Let me be master of the Straits for six hours,' he said, 'and we shall be master of the world!'

Unfortunately for him, a large British fleet remained too close at hand to risk invasion, at least for the present. Instead, Napoleon decided to attack the armies of Austria and Russia, which had joined Britain in the war against him. With amazing speed he marched his army away from the Channel and down the

River Rhine. In October came news that Admiral Nelson had defeated the main French fleet at the Battle of Trafalgar, so putting paid to any invasion of Britain. Undeterred, Napoleon defeated an Austrian force at the German city of Ulm, near the Black Forest. From there he advanced with his courageous

Napoleon fought the Russian and Austrian armies all day at the Battle of Austerlitz, finally winning despite many deaths on both sides.

soldiers to Vienna.

On 2 December 1805, the first anniversary of his coronation, Napoleon met a combined Austrian and Russian army at Austerlitz (now in Czechoslovakia). Between dawn and dusk of that brief winter's day he fought an army far larger than his own, killing or capturing nearly 30,000 of the enemy soldiers and hundreds of guns. The Battle of Austerlitz was his most stunning victory.

The city of light

In the next three years, Napoleon destroyed the other forces of the coalition lined up against him. He and his marshals defeated the Prussian army at Jena and Auerstadt (1806), and the Russians at Eylau and Friedland, now both in Poland (1807). When the Austrians challenged him again, he beat them once more, at Wagram, near Vienna (1809). On land, at least, Napoleon seemed unbeatable. He was master of nearly the whole of continental Europe, from northern Germany

The Arc de Triomphe, a memorial to Napoleon's great army.

The Madeleine Church was begun in Napoleon's day.

to southern Italy, from Poland to the Pyrenees.

Napoleon decided that Paris should become the political and cultural capital of the world. He built new bridges over the River Seine, rebuilt the beautiful Rue de Rivoli, enlarged the Louvre Museum to house treasures from Egypt and other parts of his empire, and began work on both the Madeleine Church and the colossal Arc de Triomphe, as memorials to his great army. He also introduced gas lighting, one of the wonders of the age, to his 'city of light'.

Napoleon was also as determined as ever to create his own dynasty to rule over Europe. He made his brothers kings or princes of different parts of his empire. Above all, he wanted a son and heir to his own title of Emperor. He had not produced any children with his wife Josephine, so he divorced her and married the young Princess Marie Louise of Austria, a member of the ancient royal house of Hapsburg. In 1811 she bore Napoleon a son. He joyfully ordered a salute of 101 guns to celebrate the event. He hoped a Napoleon would rule over Europe for generations to come.

Napoleon was delighted that his new wife had given him a son.

Fortunes in the balance

The French and Russians met head on at the Battle of Borodino.

Only one problem cast a shadow over this triumphant period of Napoleon's life—France was still at war with Britain. Napoleon waged a type of economic warfare, by ordering all the countries of continental Europe to stop trading with Britain. When Spain and Portugal ignored this policy, he sent in an army of occupation. Britain thereupon dispatched its own force, commanded by Sir Arthur Wellesley (soon to become the Duke of Wellington).

It was the start of the Peninsular War, with the British, aided by Spanish and Portuguese guerrillas, holding down 200,000 French troops.

At the other end of Europe, the Russian Tsar Alexander I had also defied the French ban on trade with Britain. So Napoleon decided he must also act against Russia. In the spring of 1812 he assembled his biggest army yet, with contingents from all over his empire, spearheaded by the faithful troops of his Imperial

Guard, creating altogether a strong force of well over 400,000 men.

In June 1812 they invaded Russia. The Russian army was, to begin with, poorly organized and equipped. But they had the advantage of being on home ground. The further Napoleon and his army advanced across the vast Russian plains, the more problems they had with supplies and communications. At the Battle of Borodino, the Russians met the French head on. Napoleon called it 'the most terrible of all my battles'. Much weakened, his army still managed to reach Moscow. There Napoleon hoped to meet the Tsar. Instead, he found the Russian capital largely deserted and in flames. There was nothing for him to do but retreat again.

The Russians deserted Moscow and set it alight so that there was nothing left for Napoleon's army.

Retreat and defeat

Napoleon left a large part of his army behind in Russia, as he had done years before in Egypt. The remainder set out with him on the long trek back. The weather, in October 1812, was kind at first. Then the temperature suddenly fell, and it began to snow. Few of the men had winter clothing and soon they were suffering from exposure and frostbite. Napoleon himself often trudged along with them through the snow—it was warmer than sitting on a horse. The cold, half-starved troops were afraid to sleep at night, because of the danger from wolves. The Russian soldiers attacked them by day, dashing without warning out of the forests to slash to pieces any sick stragglers. Thousands perished in the terrible retreat.

Napoleon, protected by his Imperial Guard, reached Poland,

and from there rushed back to Paris, to restore his authority and rethink his strategy. He still controlled large areas of Europe, with all their resources of men and materials. The Austrians were also still subdued, and he hoped to do a deal with them. He mustered another army, and in May 1813 beat the Russians and Prussians at Lutzen in Germany.

It was not enough to stem the tide of events. In June, news reached him that Wellington had won a big victory at Vittoria, in Spain. This heartened the Austrians, who joined the new alliance of Russia and Prussia. In October 1813, in the tremendous three-day Battle of Leipzig (The Battle of the Nations), the allies defeated the French through sheer weight of numbers. With the Russians, Prussians and Austrians now heading towards the Rhine from the east, and the British moving up to the Pyrenees from Spain, Napoleon and France were in great danger.

The cruel Russian winter claimed the lives of many of Napoleon's soldiers.

The Hundred Days

Napoleon is bid farewell as he leaves the Palace of Fontainebleau.

In the winter of 1813–14, the armies of the coalition invaded France. Napoleon fought some brilliant defensive actions, but he could not prevent the capture of Paris by the Russians and Prussians. His own position suddenly collapsed.

Talleyrand, who had helped Napoleon gain power and had served him as foreign minister, now led the opposition against him. Talleyrand forced Napoleon to abdicate and restored a member of the old French royal family to the throne. At the Palace of Fontainebleau, south of the capital, Napoleon took a famous farewell of his marshals and the Imperial Guard, and left for exile on the Mediterranean island of Elba, not far from Corsica. Talleyrand, meanwhile, joined the other leaders of Europe at the Congress of Vienna, to settle the future now that Napoleon had gone.

Napoleon, however, was not finished yet. Encouraged by reports that the new French King Louis XVIII was unpopular, he escaped from Elba and in March 1815 landed secretly near Cannes on the south coast of France. His journey back to Paris, gathering support all the way, was a triumph. With Talleyrand in Vienna, King Louis lost his nerve and fled. The people of Paris turned out in their thousands to welcome Napoleon back. It was the start of the last brief but dramatic chapter of his career, from April to June 1815—the 'Hundred Days'.

Exiled to Elba, Napoleon planned his escape.

Waterloo

Napoleon acted quickly to break the new coalition formed against him. Despite the huge losses of men in Spain, Russia and elsewhere, he was still able to conscript a big new army. Early in June 1815, he advanced with it into Belgium, to face one army of British, Dutch and Hanoverian troops, commanded by the Duke of Wellington, and a second, Prussian army, led by General Blücher. He attacked the Prussians first, at Ligny, driving them eastwards with heavy losses. Then he prepared to face Wellington's army at Waterloo, near Brussels, confident of victory.

The Battle of Waterloo, 18 June 1815, was preceded by a

thunderstorm, which soaked the soldiers on both sides. Napoleon waited for the ground to dry, before opening the battle with a great artillery barrage. Led by Marshal Ney, who had played a major role in so many of Napoleon's earlier campaigns, the French then launched their cavalry against Wellington's infantry, while their own infantry fought for key positions on the battlefield. Slowly but surely, they were gaining ground. Then, at about 7.30 pm,

Above *Wellington and Blücher meet at Waterloo.*

Left *Napoleon at Waterloo.*

Blücher and his Prussians, recovered from their defeat, rode in from the east. Wellington, suddenly sensing victory, waved his hat as a signal for a general advance. The French line, now outflanked by the Prussians, wavered, and broke.

Napoleon fled from the battlefield, where over 60,000 men lay dead or dying.

Exile and death

Napoleon was allowed three officers and twelve servants on St Helena. Here he dictates a letter to one of his officers (left).

'My political life is over,' Napoleon wrote a few days after Waterloo, 'and I proclaim my son as Emperor of the French with the title of Napoleon II.'

It was a hopeless gesture.

Within weeks he was on his way to a new exile, this time on the lonely island of St Helena in the South Atlantic Ocean, and Louis XVIII was back once again as King of France. Napoleon remained a prisoner on St Helena for another six years, where he died, after a painful illness, on 21 May 1821. He was still only 52 years old.

It seemed, at first, as though the world had forgotten him. With the Congress of Vienna, the old kingdoms of Europe and the 'balance of power', were restored. But at a deeper level, Napoleon had shaped the real future. As a general he had conscripted larger armies, and moved them with more speed, than anyone had previously dreamed of doing. His tactics set the pattern for modern war. As a statesman and politician, he had created the first modern state, with a strong central government and an efficient civil service controlling all important aspects of life.

In 1840 his remains were brought back to France from St Helena and placed in a giant stone tomb in the Palace of Les Invalides, a home for old soldiers, in Paris. By then everybody, whether they approved of him or not, agreed that Napeoleon was one of the greatest military and political leaders who had ever lived.

Napoleon's remains were brought back to France and placed in this giant tomb.

Important events

1769   Napoleon Buonaparte born at Ajaccio, Corsica.

1789   Storming of the Bastille and the start of the French Revolution.

1793   As an artillery officer, Napoleon helps to recapture Toulon from British and royalist forces. Promoted to brigadier.

1795   He suppresses royalist uprising in Paris. Promoted to general.

1796–7   Marries Josephine Beauharnais. Embarks on Italian campaign, and wins first big victory at Rivoli.

1798   Egyptian campaign and battles of the Pyramids and Aboukir Bay.

1800   Napoleon takes over government of France as First Consul. Introduces many political reforms. Leads second Italian campaign and wins Battle of Marengo.

1802   Peace treaty (at Amiens) brings temporary end to war with Britain.

1803   Britain leads a new coalition against France.

1804   Napoleon crowned Emperor of the French.

1805   Napoleon abandons plans to invade Britain, loses naval Battle of Trafalgar, but defeats Austrians at Ulm and Austerlitz.

1806–7   Defeats the Prussians at Jena and Auerstadt, and the Russians at Eylau and Friedland.

1808   Wellington leads a British force against the French in Spain and Portugal. Start of Peninsular War.

1809   Napoleon defeats the Austrians again at Wagram. Divorces Josephine and marries Princess Marie Louise of Austria.

1812   Napoleon invades Russia, wins Battle of Borodino, but is forced to retreat from Moscow.

1813   Wellington wins Battle of Vittoria in Spain. Napoleon defeats Russians and Prussians at Lutzen but loses Battle of Leipzig.

1814   Coalition armies invade France. Napoleon abdicates, and is exiled to island of Elba. The Congress of Vienna.

1815   Napoleon returns from Elba. 'The Hundred Days' ends in defeat at Battle of Waterloo. Napoleon exiled to island of St Helena.

1821   Napoleon dies on St Helena.

Glossary

Abdicate To renounce the title of emperor, kind or other position of leadership.

Artillery Troops specialized in using cannon.

Coalition A group of nations, or political parties, forming a union or alliance.

Colony A country or territory developed by another nation and controlled by it.

Conscript Someone enlisted to serve in an organization, usually an army. The opposite of a volunteer.

Constitution Rules or conventions concerning the government of a country and the rights and duties of citizens.

Dynasty A succession of rulers, usually belonging to the same family.

Exile Forced removal or expulsion of someone from their own country.

Guerrilla Spanish word meaning 'little war', describing a type of soldier acting on his own, or as part of a small independent group.

Referendum An election dealing with one special issue.

Republic A nation headed usually by an elected president rather than by a hereditary monarch.

Strategy The overall plan of campaign in a war, as distinct from tactics, which are concerned with individual battles.

Books to read

Napoleon by Augustin Drouet (Granada, 1981)

Spotlight on the Age of Revolution by Michael Gibson (Wayland, 1985)

The Napoleonic Wars by Michael Glover (Batsford, 1979)

Napoleon by Anthony Masters (Longman, 1981)

The Story of Napoleon by L. Du Garde Peach (Ladybird, 1968)

Napoleon Bonaparte by Brian Williams (Ward Lock, 1979)

Index

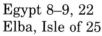

32